PRAYER STRIKE

A DEEP DIVE INTO ELECTRIFYING INTERCESSION

ELVENA MCCAIN

Prayer Strike

© 2023 Elvena McCain

This is a Revised and Expanded Edition of Operation Prayer Strike:

Copyright © 2016 – Robert Hotchkin and Patricia King

CONTENTS

Introduction

PRAYER STRIKE VISION AND PURPOSE

Our vision is to see the whole earth filled with the Glory of God through powerful prayers and intercession, shifting the atmosphere of Nations. Our purpose is to equip, train, and "arm" God's people with the power and authority He has given us.

WHAT IS INTERCESSION?

Definition: "To go or pass between; to act between parties with a view to reconcile those who differ or contend; to interpose; to mediate or make intercession; mediation." (Websters Dictionary)

1. **"STANDING IN THE GAP" – CHRIST'S POSITION IN THE HEAVENLIES**

    – Intercessor - Hebrews 7:24-28

    – Mediator - 1 Timothy 2:5

    – Advocate - 1 John 2:1

2. **"PAGA" - FROM STRONG'S CONCORDANCE #6293 (VERB)**

    – "Make intercession"

    – "Intercessor"

    – "To make attack"

    – "To meet-join"

    – "To light upon"

    – "To strike"

    – "To reach (hit) the mark"

JAMES 5:16

The effectual fervent payer of a righteous man avails much.

EZEKIEL 22:30 - 1 TIMOTHY 2:1 (VERSIONS)

And I sought for a man among them that should make up the hedge, and stand in the gap before me for the land, that I should not destroy it: But I found none.....I exhort therefore, that, first of all, supplications, prayers and intercessions, and giving of thanks, be made for all men.

THE CROSS

Hebrews 12:2
"Looking unto Jesus, the author and finisher of our faith, who for the joy that was set before Him endured the cross, despising the shame, and has set down at the right hand of the throne of God."

1. THE COVENANT OF LOVE

- John 3:16; John 15:13; 1John 3:1; Romans 8:31-39

2. MAN HAD TO DIE - ROMANS 6:23

- a. Jesus became our representative and substitute. John 3:16

- b. Jesus became sin. 2 Corinthians 5:21

- c. Jesus died in His flesh for man. 1 Peter 3:18

- Through Christ, man is dead to sin, the flesh and the world.

- Galatians 6:14; Romans 6:7-12; Romans 8

3. THE CROSS DESTROYED THE ENMITY BETWEEN GOD AND MAN

- Colossians 2:14; Ephesians 2:16

—NOTES—

LESSON ONE

Faith

Faith is the "connector" which secures the covenant blessings that were wrought through Christ's finished work on the cross, bringing them into our experiential realm. It is very important that we understand how to release our faith in order to access all that we have been given.

1.   FAITH IS OUR FOUNDATION

- We cannot please God without it. —Hebrews 11:6

- Every man has a measure of faith. —Romans 12:3

- It is the victory that overcomes the world. —1 John 5:4

- It is the substance and evidence of spiritual things. —Hebrews 11:1

- Faith creates things that are not. —Romans 4:16-25

- Faith is a force from God, given as a gift. —Mark 11:2-3; Ephesians 2:8-10

2.   OUR SALVATION IS BASED ON FAITH ALONE

- Ephesians 2:8 - Saved by grace when you believe.

- Hebrews 11:6 - Trust and believe that God exists

3.   BLESSINGS AND PROMISES ARE APPROPRIATED BY FAITH

- Ephesians 1:3 - He has Blessed us with every spiritual blessing

- 2 Peter 1:2-4 - He has Given us great and precious promises

- Romans 1:17 - God makes us right in His sight - by FAITH

4.   STEPS TO RELEASING FAITH

– **Faith hears. —Romans 10:17**

- Rhema vs. logos

– **True faith is always birthed and led by the Holy Spirit and is not "presumption."**

- Positioning yourself to hear – intimacy

– **Faith sees.**

- Genesis 13:14-15

- Habakkuk 2:1-3

– **Faith speaks. —Romans 10:8-10**

- The power of the tongue —James 3:1-12

- Your words release faith. —2 Corinthians 4:13

- From the abundance of the heart —Matthew 12:34

– **Faith rejoices.**

- 1 Thessalonians 5:16 — Always be joyful

– **Faith gives thanks.**

- 1 Thessalonians 5:18 — Be thankful in ALL circumstances.

- Matthew 15:36 — He took the loaves and fish and gave thanks.

– **Faith acts. —James 2:14-26**

- Be a doer of the Word. —James 1:22

– **Faith persists and endures. —Galatians 6:9**

- P.U.S.H. (Pray until something happens) —

- Matthew 17:20

- Abraham hoped against hope. —Romans 4:16-18

- The watchmen who take no rest —Isaiah 62:6-7

- O.T. believers who endured in faith —Hebrews 11:13

- Parable of the unjust judge —Luke 18:1-8

- Jacob persisted and prevailed. —Genesis 32:26-29

– **FAITH FIGHTS - 1 Timothy 6:12**

– **FAITH RESTS - Hebrews 4:1-12**

– **FAITH RECEIVES - Mark 11:24**

—NOTES—

LESSON TWO

HEARING FROM THE LORD

1. GOD SPEAKS TO HIS PEOPLE

- 1 Samuel 3:1-7
  The Lord speaks to Samuel.

- John 10:27
  "My sheep hear My voice and they will follow Me."

2. PREPARING YOUR HEART/HEAR FROM GOD

- Invite the Holy Spirit to convict you of any unconfessed sin.

- Commit yourself to hearing.

- Be filled with the Word; commit to daily devotional times and daily Word confessions

- Come to know the Holy Spirit in a personal way.

- Respect and awe of God and His word, with the fear of the Lord.

- Do not doubt.

- James 1:6–7: Walk by faith, not by natural senses or feelings.

- Posture yourself to hear.

- Worship

- Prayer

- Listening for Holy Spirit to speak

- Submission to leadership in a local assembly (for accountability)

- Right relationships in the Body of Christ

3.   DISCERNING GOD'S VOICE

"The voice of a stranger they will not hear..." —John 10:4-5

- **God's voice**

  - Righteous

  - Loving

  - Unto salvation

  - Full of mercy

  - Humble

  - Authoritative

  - Without condemnation

  - Truth (agrees with Scripture)

  - Life-giving

- **The voice of the flesh**

  - Self-seeking

  - Personal agenda

  - Self-exalting

  - "Soul-driven" ("Humanism")

- **The voice of the enemy (demonic)**

  - Accusative

  - Violates the Word (or twists it)

  - Leads people away from the Savior

  - Leads people away from righteousness

  - Deceptive – appeals to the flesh

  - Brings death and destruction

4.   **WHEN/HOW GOD SPEAKS**

- Still small voice (words or thoughts)

- Mental pictures or impressions (thought pictures)

- Through the Scriptures
  - Logos becomes Rhema

- Through creation

- Through trials and testings

- Audible voice

  - God's audible voice

  - Inner audible voice

  - Through other believers

  - Inspired utterance

- Dreams while we sleep

- Daydreams

  - Open-eyed vision

- Close-eyed vision

- Open-eyed "spiritual" vision

- Colors

- Symbols (i.e., animals, flowers, foods, objects)

- Emotions

- Body impressions

- Spiritual Senses

- Flashback

- Through angelic visitation

—NOTES—

LESSON THREE

ALL MANNER OF PRAYER —PART ONE

Pray at ALL times – on every occasion, in every season – in the Spirit, with all manner of prayer." —Ephesians 6:18 (AMPC)

1.   **THE PRAYER OF AGREEMENT**

Matthew 18:18-20

"Truly I say to you, whatever you bind on earth shall have been bound in heaven; and whatever you loose on earth shall have been loosed in heaven." (18:18)

– **AGREEMENT WITH HEAVEN**

"Again I say to you, that if two of you agree on earth about anything that they may ask, it shall be done for them by My Father who is in heaven." (18:19)

– **AGREEMENT WITH ONE ANOTHER**

"For where two or three have gathered together in My name, I am there in their midst." (18:20)

– **AGREEMENT WITH HIS NAME**

Mark 5:35-42
Jesus sent the mockers out of the room because they were not in AGREEMENT

Acts 4:32a
All the believers were united in heart and mind.

Acts 12:5-12
"So Peter was kept in the prison, but prayer for him was being made fervently by the church to God." (5:5)

SHORT INSTANTANEOUS PRAYER

***DISCUSS WITH CLASS**

2.   **PRAYING GOD'S WORD**

- **IT IS POWERFUL**

  Hebrews 4:12

  " For the word of God is living and active and sharper than any two-edged sword."

- **IT IS PLANTING SEED**

  Mark 4:26-32

  "And He was saying, 'The kingdom of God is like a man who casts seed upon the soil; and he goes to bed at night and gets up by day, and the seed sprouts and grows – how, he himself does not know.'" (4:26-27)

- **IT ACTIVATES ANGELS.**

  Psalm 103:20

  "Bless the Lord, you His angels, mighty in strength, who perform His word, obeying the voice of His word!"

- **ALWAYS ACCOMPLISHES ITS ASSIGNMENT**

  Isaiah 55:8-11

  "So will My word be which goes forth from My mouth. It will not return to Me empty, without accomplishing what I desire, and without succeeding in the matter for which I sent it." (55:11)

3.   THE PRAYER OF PETITION

PETITION: "a formal request, usually written down and signed; a specific request or plea in which specific court action is asked for."

1 Samuel 1:27

"For this boy I prayed, and the Lord has given me my petition which I asked of Him."

Esther 5:7,8

"So Esther replied, 'My petition and my request is: if I have found favor in the sight of the king, and if it pleases the king to grant my petition and do what I request.' "

4.   PRAYER OF SUPPLICATION

Definition: to approach for a favor. - make a humble request.

1 Timothy 2:1
"Therefore I exhort first of all that supplications, prayers, intercessions, and giving of thanks be made for all men." (NKJV)

1 Timothy 5:5

"Now she who is really a widow, and left alone, trusts in God and continues in supplications and prayers night and day." (NKJV)

5.   PRAYERS-COMMITMENT/DEDICATION/CONSECRATION

Psalm 37:5

"Commit your way to the Lord. Trust also in Him, and He shall bring it to pass."

Proverbs 16:3

"Commit your works to the Lord, and your thoughts will be established."
(NKJV)

Joshua 3:5

"Then Joshua said to the people, 'Consecrate yourselves, for tomorrow the Lord will do wonders among you.' "

Exodus 28:41

"For Aaron's sons…..and you shall anoint them and ordain them and consecrate them that they may serve Me as priests."

1 Samuel 1:26-28

"She said, 'Oh my lord! As your soul lives, my lord, I am the woman who stood here beside you, praying to the Lord. For this boy I prayed, and the Lord has given me my petition which I asked of Him.. So I have dedicated him to the Lord; as long as he lives he is dedicated to the Lord.' And he worshiped the Lord there."

Romans 12:1

"Therefore I urge you, brethren, by the mercies of God, to present your bodies a living and holy sacrifice."

—NOTES—

ALL MANNER OF
PRAYER—PART TWO

6. GROANINGS

Romans 8:26

"In the same way the Spirit also helps our weakness; for we do not know how to pray as we should, but the Spirit Himself intercedes for us with groanings too deep for words." THE HOLY SPIRIT GROANS

Romans 8:19-22

"For the anxious longing of creation waits eagerly for the revealing of the sons of God ... For we know that the whole creation groans and suffers the pains of childbirth together until now." CREATION GROANS

Romans 8:23

"Also we ourselves, having the first fruits of the Spirit, even we ourselves groan within ourselves, waiting eagerly......" WE GROAN

Exodus 2:24

"So God heard their groaning; and God remembered His covenant with Abraham, Isaac, and Jacob."

Psalm 102:19-20

"For He looked down from His holy height; from heaven the Lord gazed upon the earth, to hear the groaning of the prisoner, to set free those who were doomed to death." GOD ANSWERS GROANINGS

7. ROARINGS

Joel 3:16 — Amos 1:2

"The Lord roars from Zion and utters His voice from Jerusalem, and the heavens and the earth tremble." THE LORD ROARS

Matthew 27:45-46a

"Now from the sixth hour until the ninth hour there was darkness over all the land. And about the ninth hour Jesus cried out with a loud voice."

Matthew 27:50a

And Jesus cried out again with a loud voice, and yielded up His spirit.

Psalm 22:1

"My God, my God, why hast thou forsaken me? Why art thou so far from helping me, and from the words of my roaring?" JESUS ROARED

Revelation 10:1-4

"I saw another strong angel coming down out of heaven ... He placed his right foot on the sea and his left on the land; and he cried out with a loud voice, as when a lion roars; and when he had cried out, the seven peals of thunder uttered their voices." THUNDER ROARS

8.   WEEPING, WAILING AND MOURNING

- **WEEPING**

    - John 11:33-35; Luke 19:41-44

        - For salvation, warfare, miracles

    - Jeremiah 9:1,10

        - For remorse prior to judgment or following judgment

    - Psalm 51:17; Psalm 34:18; Isaiah 57:18

        - Produce brokenness and contrition

    - Psalm 126:5,6

        - Cleansing through tears and for souls (beliefnet.com)

- **WAILING AND MOURNING**

  - Jeremiah 9:17,18

    - Wailers and mourners

  - Matthew 5:4

    - Blessed are those who mourn.

9.   **INTERCESSORY PRAISE**

- **PRAYERS OF SONG**

  - Psalm 7 - I will sing praise to the name of the Lord

  - Matthew 21:9 - The crowds were singing...Hosanna in the highest.

- **PRAYERS OF DANCE**

  - 1 Samuel 6:14 - And David was dancing before the Lord with all his might

  - Exodus 15:20 - Miriam the prophetess...and all the women went after her with timbrels and with dancing.

  - Judges 11:34 - Jephthah's daughter danced before her victorious father.

  - 1 Samuel 18:6 - The women danced and sang when David defeated the Philistine

—NOTES—

LESSON FOUR

DOMINION POWER

1.   WHAT IS DOMINION?

The ruling power of the King over the area/region where the King has established the boundaries of his Kingdom. In this Kingdom, the King has full dominion.

2.   GOD WANTS TO ESTABLISH HIS PEOPLE IN THE EARTH IN DOMINION AUTHORITY

This has always been the plan.

Genesis 1:26

"Let us make man in Our image, according to Our likeness; let them have DO-MINION over and all the earth.

RAW=DAW = Prevail against, reign

Psalm 8:6

You have made him to have DOMINION over the works of Your hands. You have put all things under his feet.

MAW-SHAL = "Rule, reign, have power"

Genesis 1:28

God tells Adam to "SUBDUE" the earth and rule over creation.
- *KABASH* = "CONQUER ... establish DOMINION"

Genesis 9:1

After the flood God establishes NOAH and his family as His people in the earth. He tells them to be fruitful, multiply and REPLENISH the earth.

MAN-LAY = "FULFILL ... the original plan of DOMINION"

Genesis 35:11

God transforms JACOB into ISRAEL and established a new people in the carth...He tells them to "Fill the earth, I will give it to you

NAW-THAN = "Make it yours ... TAKE dominion"

3.   GOD HAS ALWAYS WANTED A PEOPLE/RELATIONSHIP

– From RELATIONSHIP He wants His people to advance the Kingdom in the earth by walking in DOMINION

– The Promise is IMMANUEL — God is WITH YOU. It is NOT GOD who establishes His government—-it is God WITH YOU, giving us the DOMIN-ION to establish His government in the earth.

– Jesus (the Second Adam) comes to establish a new people/family for God on the earth through the cross.

4.   WE ARE THAT NEW PEOPLE/FAMILY TODAY****

– We can be that tribe/people He has always wanted and never had before by being willing to let Him do it THROUGH US and by submitting our will to His.

– GOD WANTS TO ESTABLISH **US** IN THE EARTH

– He wants US to walk in HIS DOMINION AUTHORITY !!

– He wants US to make all things new around us!

Isaiah 55:11

"So is my word that goes out from My mouth; it will not return to me empty, but will accomplish what I desire and achieve, the purpose for which I have sent it."......US TOO!!

Isaiah 60:1

"Arise, shine for your (OUR) light has come and the glory of the Lord rises upon you.......(WHOSE GLORY?)....HIS!

—NOTES—

LESSON FIVE

PROPHETIC INTERCESSION

ACTS 2:17,18

"And it shall come to pass in the last days, saith God, I will pour out of my Spirit upon all flesh: and your sons and you daughters shall prophesy, and your young men shall see visions, and your old men shall dream dreams; And on my servants and on my handmaidens I will pour out in those days of my Spirit; and they shall prophesy."

1.   PARTNER WITH GOD IN PRAYER

Matthew 16: 17,19
The Lord speaks to us so that we might declare it, and through this we become "gatekeepers," releasing heaven into the earth.

Jeremiah 33:3
"Call to Me and I will answer you, and I will tell you great and mighty things which YOU DO NOT KNOW

2.   DECLARE HIS WORD

Amos 3:7

"Surely the Lord GOD does nothing unless He reveals His secret counsel to His servants."

Jeremiah 1:5-10

"I have appointed you My spokesman to the nations." (1:5)

"Everywhere I send you, you shall go. And all that I command you, you shall speak." (1:7)

"Do not be afraid...for I am with you." (1:8)

" Behold, I have put My words in your mouth." (1:9)

Job 22:28

"You will also decree a thing, and it will be established for you; and light will shine on your ways."

3.   PREPARING TO HEAR FROM GOD

–   John 10:27 - Believe that the lord wants to speak to you.

–   Hebrews 11:6 - Approach God in faith believing that you will receive.

–   John 4:23 - Praise and Worship—will bring you into focus.

•   Ps 66:18; 139:23,24 - Invite the Holy Spirit to convict you of unconfessed sin.

•   Prov. 3:5,6; Isa. 55:8 - Lay down your own thoughts, imaginations, burdens.

–   Luke 10:19 - In Jesus' name bind the devil from hindering.

–   Eph. 5:18; John 14:26 - Invite the Holy Spirit to fill you and to speak.

4.   WAYS TO HEAR FROM GOD

–   Word or thought comes into your mind

–   Quickening of a scripture passage or verse

–   Mental picture or impression

–   Vision — a. open eye   b. Open eye spiritual.   c. Closed eye   d. Trance

–   Dreams — a. Night visions. b. Day dreams

–   Audible voice

–   Body impression

–   Flashback

–   Inner witness

–   Spiritual senses (hear, smell, taste, see, touch)

—NOTES—

LESSON SIX

THE POWER OF TONGUES

1.   **WHAT IS THE GIFT OF TONGUES?**

    —   **It is the God-given ability to speak in one or more languages that you have never learned and that you do not understand.**

    —   **The gift is under the control of the person speaking, yet completely inspired by the Holy Spirit.**

    —   **When you pray in tongues, YOUR spirit is praying.**

        1 Corinthians 14:4

        "One who speaks in a tongue edifies himself; but one who prophesies edifies the church."

    —   **The tongue is unknown to the person speaking it.**

        1 Corinthians 14:2

        "For one who speaks in a tongue does not speak to men but to God; for no one understands, but in his spirit he speaks mysteries."

        1 Corinthians 14:14

        "For if I pray in tongues, my spirit is praying, but I don't understand what I am saying."

    —   **Diverse tongues**

        1 Corinthians 12:10

        "And to another ... various kinds of tongues."

2.   THE PURPOSE OF TONGUES

– To edify yourself

1 Corinthians 14:4

"One who speaks in a tongue edifies himself; but one who prophesies edifies the church."

– For intercession and prayers

Romans 8:26-27

"In the same way the Spirit also helps our weakness; for we do not know how to pray as we should, but the Spirit Himself intercedes for us with groanings too deep for words; and He who searches the hearts knows what the mind of the Spirit is, because He intercedes for the saints according to the will of God."

– For purification

Matthew 3:11-12

"As for me, I baptize you with water for repentance, but He who is coming after me is mightier than I, and I am not fit to remove His sandals; He will baptize you with the Holy Spirit and fire. His winnowing fork is in His hand, and He will thoroughly clear His threshing floor; and He will gather His wheat into the barn, but He will burn up the chaff with unquenchable fire."

– For rest

Isaiah 28:11-12

"For with stammering lips and another tongue He will speak to this people, to whom He said, 'This is the rest with which you may cause the weary to rest,' and, 'This is the refreshing.'" (NKJV)

– For worship

John 4:23-24

"But an hour is coming, and now is, when the true worshipers will worship the Father in spirit and truth; for such people the Father seeks to be His worshipers. God is spirit, and those who worship Him must worship in spirit and truth."

    – **For edification of the assembly (tongues and interpretation)**

1 Corinthians 14:5

"Now I wish that you all spoke in tongues, but even more that you would prophesy; and greater is one who prophesies than one who speaks in tongues, unless he interprets, so that the church may receive edifying."

    – **For a sign**

Mark 16:17

"These signs will accompany those who have believed: in My name they will cast out demons, they will speak with new tongues."

1 Corinthians 14:22

"So you see that speaking in tongues is a sign, not for believers, but for unbelievers." (NLT)

    – **Proclaiming the mysteries of Christ**

1 Corinthians 14:2

"For one who speaks in a tongue does not speak to men but to God; for no one understands, but in his spirit he speaks mysteries."

3.   HOW TO RECEIVE TONGUES

    – First evidenced on the day of Pentecost — Acts 2:1-4

    – BY FAITH RECEIVE

    – BY FAITH ACT

Inspired utterance

Gift of the discerning of spirits

WAIT….LISTEN….TAKE NOTES!!

—NOTES—

LESSON SEVEN

BIRTHING PRAYER

1. EVERYTHING IS BIRTHED IN PRAYER

– **Everything of the Kingdom is birthed into the earth because someone has had a revelation of a promise of God and refused anything but its fulfillment.**

– **Beginning with Creation itself**

Genesis 1:3-26

Then God said....when we pray and say the words of God we BIRTH His will into existence. This pertains to every word He speaks to us.

Mark 11:23-24

"Truly I say to you, whoever says to this mountain, 'Be taken up and cast into the sea,' and does not doubt in his heart, but believes that what he says is going to happen, it will be granted him. Therefore I say to you, all things for which you pray and ask, believe that you have received them, and they will be granted you."

– **When you PRAY, know the PROMISE and know your PROMISER!!**

Luke 1:28-33

"May it be unto me as you have spoken." Mary's response   to Angel Gabriel. Receive your promise...trust God the HE is faithful to fulfill it THROUGH YOU....give Him your YES!! Continue praying to bring about birthing.

Isaiah 66:9

"Do I bring to the moment of birth and not give delivery? Says the Lord. Do I close up the womb when I bring to delivery?"

DECREE and DECLARE His Word. Remember He gives the promise and He will birth it through you. BE PATIENT!

2.   SIGNS OF BIRTHING

Romans 8:26b

"But the Holy Spirit prays for us with groaning that cannot be expressed in words." Holy Spirit gives us   groaning that bring forth what we do not even yet know.

Micah 4:10a

"Writhe and groan like a woman in labor." Writhing and groaning may look or sound like:

– Tears of sorrow or joy

– Laughter

– Inner and outer intimate weeping

– Groaning

– Wailing

– Travailing

– Deep rocking while praying in tongues

– Fast paced pacing while praying in tongues

– Hot "coals"in your spirit (burning sensation)

BIRTHING PRAYER……..is not something that is planned!! It simply comes upon you when the Spirit moves because you have given your YES…..you have given your "May it be unto me as you have spoken."

—NOTES—

LESSON EIGHT

CALLING DOWN THE FIRE

1.   **INTRODUCTION**

–   **Coming Move of God**

Will be marked by the "fire" of God

Hebrews 12:27-29

*"Now this, "Yet once more," indicates the removal of those things that are being shaken, as of things that are made, that the things which cannot be shaken may remain. Therefore, since we are receiving a kingdom which cannot be shaken, let us have grace, by which we may serve God acceptably with reverence and godly fear. **For our God is a consuming fire.**" (NKJV)*

2.   **MENTIONS OF BELIEVERS CALLING DOWN THE FIRE**

–   **Luke 9:51-56**

•   James and John want to call down fire on the Samaritans.

"Lord should we order down fire from heaven to burn them up as Elijah did?"

•   Jesus rebukes them.

He doesn't say, "You **can't** call down the fire..."

Nor does He say, "No, no, **don't** call down the fire..."

He says, "You do not know what spirit you are of. For the Son of Man has not come to destroy men's lives, but to save them."

- The fire of God is not a fire of wrath (in anger and offense).

- The fire of God is a FIRE OF LOVE that burns up the enemy (not man) and the things that would steal visitation/encounter (RELA-TIONSHIP) with the Lord from man.

- **1 Kings 18-20-40**

  - Elijah models this for us in the Old Testament. (1 Kings 18-20-40)

  - Elijah prays that God will answer his prayers to send the fire so that the people will know that He is God and has brought them back to Him.

    - He declares the certain heart of God toward the people.

    - As he "operates" from that, the fire falls.

    - The people are impacted by the "display" of love and cry out, "THE LORD HE IS GOD!!" (return to relationship)

  - God overcomes the enemy with fire.

  - A nation has a revelation of God.

  - Blindness, deception, seduction and intimidation of the enemy is re-moved and people choose the Lord.

  - Fire was not sent to destroy the people but to "save" them!

3. **THE FIRE OF GOD ALWAYS INVOLVES HIS LOVE, COMPAS-SION AND DESIRE TO BRING FREEDOM TO PEOPLE**

- **Exodus 3**

  - Moses encounters the burning bush (God as Fire).

  - Moses has doubts about himself.

Exodus 3:11

"But Moses protested to God, "Who am I to appear before Pharaoh? Who am I to lead the people of Israel out of Egypt?"

- The fire (presence) of God consumes the doubts.

- That fire then ignites in Moses, and he catches fire with God's love.

- When we encounter the fire of God we are changed by it; we are consumed by that fire and the purpose of the fire. We become an expression of the fire and are fueled by it.

- Moses says **yes** to being the deliverer of Israel. He is so set ablaze with the purpose that he goes back again and again until it is so.

– **Isaiah 6**

- Isaiah encounters heaven's fire (burning coal via Seraphim), and as soon as he is touched by the fire of God he immediately wants to go and see others set free!!

- - **"SEND ME!"**

– **Acts 2 – Pentecost**

- They are touched by the fire and immediately they were outside preaching and sharing the reality of the Gospel (3,000 added to the church).

- And this is just a foretaste of what the full baptism of His fire will do.

– **Revelation 1:12-16**

- John sees the Lord as the Fiery (burning) One , and then receives seven words for the churches (as apostle of Love)

- Words (and the fire of love he now carries) are to deal with anything getting in the way of the church walking fully with God.

4.   FIRE OF GOD IS NOT TO DESTROY MAN

- **Not wrath/judgment against man**

    - It is wrath/judgment against the enemy.

    - John the Baptist tells us that Jesus is coming to baptize us with Holy Spirit **and** fire (not or fire).

        • It is not salvation/restored relationship/Holy Spirit ... or you will burn in hell.

        • It is Holy Spirit and desire for all to have it (heart of God, burning love,) that destroys all that would separate man from God.

- **Malachi 4**

    • Fire comes to purify and refine us. Then our purified hearts burn with what God's heart burns with.

5.   HOW TO CALL DOWN THE FIRE

- **The first and most important step is to connect with the heart of God for the person/place situation.........THEN:**

        • TAKE THE TIME TO REALLY RECEIVE HIS HEART..

        • TO SEE THEM AS HE DOES

        • TO LOVE THEM AS HE DOES

- Discern the spirits that are oppressing/binding/influencing the person or place.

- Call the fire of God down upon those spirits.

- Declare the person/place's freedom from those spirits and influences.

- Declare who God is with/for that person/place and who they are with/for Him.

—NOTES—

LESSON NINE

WATCHING AND FASTING

1. **PRAYER WATCHING**

    In the days of Roman rule, the strategy of four watches, starting at 6:00 p.m., 9:00 p.m., 12:00 midnight and 3:00 a.m., was introduced.

    -   *First Watch! The Evening Watch!* The Evening watch begins at 6:00 pm —9:00 pm. This is a time that we need to "still" ourselves from the world and to meditate.

    -   *Second Watch! The Midnight Watch!* The Midnight watch begins at 9:00 pm —Midnight. This is a time for thanksgiving as well as visitation. Also expect some warfare during this watch.

    -   *Third Watch! The Breaking of the Day (Cockcrowing) Watch*! This watch begins at Midnight until 3:00 am. The focus of the previous watch continues with the additional understanding that there is much spiritual activity occurring during this time period, including our own dream realm.

    -   *Fourth Watch! The Morning Watch - A New Day Dawning!* This watch begins at 3:00 am — 6:00 am. This watch is linked with the approaching morning light and the breaking of the day. When daylight comes, your position is exposed to the eyes of the enemy BUT during this watch, you become covered with the glory of the Lord!

    -   **Scriptures:**

        -   Ezekiel 33:1-9

            "The people of the land take a man from among them and set him for their watchman."

"I have appointed you a watchman for the house ... so you will hear a message from My mouth and give them warning from Me."

- **Isaiah 62:6-7**

"On your walls, O Jerusalem, I have appointed watchmen. All day and all night they will never keep silent. You who remind the Lord, take no rest for yourselves. And give Him no rest until He establishes, and makes Jerusalem a praise in the earth."

- **Isaiah 52:8**

"Listen! Your watchmen lift up their voices. They shout joyfully together. For they will see with their own eyes when the Lord restores Zion."

- **Mark 14:33-38**

"And He said to them, 'My soul is deeply grieved to the point of death; remain here and keep watch.'"

"Could you not keep watch for one hour? Keep watching and praying that you may not come into temptation; the spirit is willing, but the flesh is weak."

- **2 Corinthians 6:4-5** (apostolic duty)

"But in everything commending ourselves as servants of God, in much endurance, in afflictions, in hardships, in distresses, in beatings, in imprisonments, in tumults, in labors, in sleeplessness, in hunger."

- **2 Corinthians 11:27 (apostolic duty)**

"I have been in labor and hardship, through many sleepless nights, in hunger and thirst, often without food, in cold and exposure."

2.   FASTING

Fasting is a total or partial abstinence from food. When we fast, we are humbling ourselves so that we might give ourselves to God in prayer to the end that we might help others in a greater way and see God's will accomplished.

- **Purpose of a fast:**

  - To humble yourself (Psalm 35:13)

  - To loosen bonds of wickedness (Isaiah 58:6)

  - A time to purify our motives (Isaiah 58:9-10)

  - Sensitivity to the needs of others (Isaiah 58:7

  - To strengthen the "inner man" in order to minister to others (Matthew 17:21)

  - Focused prayer

  - For direction

- **Benefits of fasting**

  - Strength to the spirit man

  - Release of faith

  - Sensitivity to spiritual experiences (dreams, visions, etc.)

- **Types of fasts**

  - Absolute fast – no food or water (Exodus 34:28, Esther 4:16)

  - Normal fast – water but no food

  - Partial fast – abstaining from certain foods or times (Daniel 10:3)

– **What to do during a fast**

- Be specific about its purpose – declare it.

- Prayer and study of the Word

- Recognize spiritual attack.

- Personal repentance

- Avoid religious ostentation (Matthew 6:16).

– **Rewards of fasting (Isaiah 58:6-12)**

- Bonds of wickedness broken

- Physical healing

- Righteousness and glory manifested

- Answered prayer

- Freedom from depression

- Guidance from the Lord

- Fulfillment

- Renewed physical strength

- Prosperity

- Restoration of people's lives

—NOTES—

LESSON TEN

PRAYING FOR CITIES, NATIONS AND REGIONS

1.   **WE CAN SPEAK TO CITIES AND NATIONS AND COMMAND THEM TO ALIGN WITH GOD'S TRUTH**

   – *Matthew 23:37,38*

   "O Jerusalem, Jerusalem how I long to gather YOUR people..."

   • JESUS spoke to cities

   – *Psalm 24:7*

   He commanded the spirit gates of his city to open up and receive the King of Glory! David spoke a COMMAND over his city.

   – *Jeremiah 1:9,10*

   "Then the Lord reached out and touched my mouth and said, 'Look I have put my words in your mouth! Today I appoint you to stand up against nations and Kingdoms. Some you must uproot and tear down, destroy and overthrow. Others you must build up and plant."

   ** WE SHOULD MEMORIZE THIS SCRIPTURE!! God is sending us to PLACES, putting His Words in our mouth to tear down darkness and build up places/things of light.

   – *Isaiah 55:5*

   "You also will command nations you do not know, and peoples unknown to you will come running to obey, because I, the Lord your God, the Holy One of Israel, have made you glorious."

   • When we walk in this TRUTH we will see cities, nations and regions START TO SHIFT!

– *Isaiah 60:3*

NATIONS will come to your light, and KINGS to the brightness of your dawn....

2.   OUR STRATEGIES

– Scouting out the land (spiritual mapping)

– Documenting and journaling - KEY to get God's strategy

– Decreeing and establishing the Word of God

– Spiritual Warfare as directed by Holy Spirit

3.   CONQUERING THE GATES

– GEOGRAPHICAL GATES - Regions

– SPIRITUAL GATES - Individual souls or..CYBER SPACE

– POLITICAL GATES - Isaiah 9:6, Government rests on His shoulders

– ECONOMIC GATES - Kingdom currency - Faith Giving

– EDUCATION GATES - Prayer back in schools

– MEDIA GATES - Division, deception, lies

– ARTS & ENTERTAINMENT GATES - Morality, purity, righteousness

– MARRIAGE & FAMILY GATES - Adultery, divorce, abortion

4.   **ESTABLISHING THE KINGDOM OF GOD**

— *Psalm 2:8*
Ask of Me, and I will surely give the nations as your inheritance and the very ends of the earth as your possession.

— *Psalm 33:12*
Blessed is the nation whose God is the Lord, the people Whom He has CHOSEN for His own inheritance.

— *Proverbs 14:34*
Righteousness exalts a nation, but sin is a disgrace to any people.

— *Proverbs 21:1 - 1 Timothy 2:1,2*

SCRIPTURES TO PRAY FOR GOVERNMENT AND LEADERS OF NATIONS AND CITIES

5.   **PRAYER INITIATIVES**

— United prayer (prayer gatherings & meetings)

— Leadership (ministerial prayer)

— Prayer walks and drives

— Prophetic decrees and actions over cities and nations

—NOTES—

LESSON ELEVEN

WARFARE PRAYER
Part One

1.` **INTRODUCTION**

- Spiritual warfare enforces the victory of Calvary. Victory is already accomplished, but we need to lay hold of that victory.

- Sometimes this involves confrontation with the enemy.

    • We need to resist him. (James 4:7)

    • We are not to be **ignorant** of Satan's schemes. (2 Cor 2:11)

        • **"ignorant"** - "agneo - without knowledge or understanding.

        • **"schemes"** - "nosema" - thoughts, plans, schemes, plots.

        • **"advantage"** - "pleonekteo" - to have or hold a greater position, to make a gain, to make pay of, to defraud, that no advantage would be taken of us by Satan, for we are not ignorant of his schemes"

2. **BIBLICAL FACTS ABOUT WARFARE**

- **We are in spiritual warfare.**

    2 Corinthians 10:3-4; 1 Tim 1:18

    –   **We are called as soldiers to fight and to wrestle**.

          2 Timothy 2:3-4; Eph 6:10-12

    –   We are to tread upon the enemy and his works.

          Luke 10:19; Romans 16:20

    –   We are equipped with armor and weapons

          2 Corinthians 10:3-5; Ephesians 6:10-18

    –   We are seated in heavenly places in Christ.

          Ephesians 1:5–2:6

    –   We have authority to bind and to loose.

          Matthew 16:19

3.   THE CLASH OF THE KINGDOMS

    –   The kingdom of light
          Matthew 12:22 - 28

          The kingdom of darkness
          Ephesians 6:10-12

4.   LANDING STRIPS FOR THE ENEMY

    –   Deuteronomy 28:15-68

        •   Disobedience (28:15, 58)

        •   Not keeping His commands and ways

        •   Not serving the Lord with joy and a glad heart (28:47)

        •   No fear of the Lord (28:58)

– Romans 6:16

"Do you not know that when you present yourselves to someone as slaves for obedience, you are slaves of the one whom you obey, either of sin resulting in death, or of obedience resulting in righteousness?"

– 2 Chronicles 7:14

"And My people who are called by My name humble themselves and pray and seek My face and turn from their wicked ways, then I will hear from heaven, will forgive their sin and will heal their land."

4.   DISCERNING OF SPIRITS (1 CORINTHIANS 12:10)

– Visions and mental images

– Inner sensings

– Words or thoughts

– Body impressions

– Observing outward manifestations (fruit)

—NOTES—

WARFARE PRAYER

Part Two

5. WARFARE PRAYER

- **Mountain moving prayer/authoritative prayer**

  Mark 11:23-24; Isa 41:15; Isa 40-4

- **First recorded instance of the disciples using the name of Jesus**

  Acts 3:1-10

- **Know your covenant!**
  - David vs. Goliath 1 Samuel 17

- **Enforcing the victory**

  Psalm 110:2,3

  As we involve ourselves in spiritual warfare, it is important to realize that we are not trying to defeat the devil. He is already defeated. We do not re-defeat him. We secure the victory of Calvary. The victory has already been accomplished in the heavenlies, we simply secure it in our hearts and into the earth.

- **Decreeing the wisdom of God**

  Ephesians 3:8-10

- **Signs of conquest:**
  - Subduing our enemies
    - Psalm 18:39-40

- Taking the necks of our enemies
    - Joshua 10:22-27

- **Crushing the head of the enemy**

    - Genesis 3:15; Romans 16:20

        Hebrew "bruise" = *shuwph* = "to bruise, crush, shatter"

        Hebrew "head" = *rosh* = "headship or authority"

        Greek "crush" = suntribo = to trample, to break in pieces, to shatter, bruise, grind down, smash

6. **WEAPONS OF WARFARE (NON-EXHAUSTIVE)**
    - **The Word of God**
        Hebrews 4:12

    - **The Name of Jesus**
        Mark 16:17; Philippians 2:9-11

    - **Praise and worship**
        2 Chronicles 20:20-25

    - **Prophetic decrees and actions**
        Isaiah 55:11

    - **Banners and flags**
        Isaiah 13:1-3; Psalm 60:4,5

    - **Dance**
        1 Samuel 18:6

– **The gifts of the Spirit**

   1 Corinthians 12:7-10

– **Roars**

   Joel 3:16

– **Shouts**

   Joshua 6:16

– **Repentance**

   Matthew 3:2

– **The blood of Jesus**

   Revelation 12:11

– **Laughter**

   Psalm 2:4

7.   PULLING DOWN STRONGHOLDS

"For the weapons of our warfare are not of the flesh, but divinely powerful for the destruction of fortresses. We are destroying speculations and every lofty thing raised up against the knowledge of God, and we are taking every thought captive to the obedience of Christ." —2Corinthians10:4-5

– **Stronghold (fortress):**

   Greek = *ochuroma* = to have or hold; a place from which to hold something strongly; a fort, castle, or prison

– **Speculations:**

   Greek = *logismos* = the sum total of accumulated information learned over time. It becomes what we really believe; a person's mindsets.

- **Lofty thing**

    Greek = *hupsoma* = any elevated place or thing (pride)

- **Thoughts**

    Greek = *noema* = plans, schemes, devices, plots

8. AGGRESSIVELY DEALING WITH THE ENEMY IN SPIRITUAL WARFARE

- Submit yourself completely to the authority of Christ and the direction of the Holy Spirit. James 4:7

- Gird up with the full armor of God. Ephesians 6:10-18

    - "the belt of truth" (6:14)

    - "the breastplate of righteousness" (6:14)

    - "shod your feet with the preparation of the gospel of peace" (6:15)

    - "shield of faith" (6:16)

    - "helmet of salvation" (6:17)

    - "sword of the Spirit, which is the word of God" (6:17)

- Destroy any legal right of the enemy through repentance and cleansing (prayer of identification – e.g., Nehemiah).

    - Nehemiah 1:1-6 (NKJV)

- Binding and loosing prayers

    - Matthew 16:19

– Bind the strongman.

    Matthew 12:29

– Pray authoritative prayers. "Mountain be thou removed"

    Mark 11:23

– Call forth the authority of the Kingdom, the power and the glory.

    Matthew 6:9-13

– Be alert for "kickbacks."

    Luke 10:19

"Behold, I have given you authority to tread on serpents and scorpions, and over all the power of the enemy, and nothing will injure you."

JESUS CHRIST IS THE VICTOR!

JESUS CHRIST IS LORD!

—NOTES—

LESSON TWELVE

THE PRAYER SHIELD

CREATING A FORTRESS OF PRAYER TO COVER AND PROTECT LEADERS! (1 Timothy 2:1-2)

A.   WHAT IS A PRAYER SHIELD?

1. Intercessors who are committed to praying for a leader/leaders.

2. Role of armor bearer (1 Samuel 16:21 and 14: 7-14)

   a. The armor bearer carried the leader's armor for them so that they would always be ready for battle.

   b. The armor bearer went before the leader, covering him with a shield that in most cases was as large as the leader.

   c. The armor bearer often fought the battles along with the leader.

   d. The armor bearer often would walk behind the leader after the battle to watch his back.

3. The release and manifestation of Jesus as the leader's "shield" through intercession. (Genesis 15:1)

4. A release of faith through prayer that operates as a shield that extinguishes all the fiery darts of the enemy. (Ephesians 6:16)

B.   WHY DOES A LEADER NEED SPIRITUAL COVERING AND PROTECTION THROUGH PRAYER?

1. The enemy targets leaders, their families, and their ministries because he knows he can destroy vision and people if he can bring down the leader.

2. In order for those who are in the realm of influence of the leader to experi-

ence peace and blessing. (1Timothy 2:1-2)

3. In order for the leader to clearly receive spiritual revelation, blessing and empowerment for service.

C. WHAT AREAS OF A LEADER'S LIFE AND MINISTRY SHOULD BE COVERED IN PRAYER?

1. Personal walk with the Lord, devotional life, and consecration to the Lord.

2. Character integrity and development (fashioned into the image of Christ)

3. Marriage and family (if applicable)

4. Wisdom

5. Development of ministry gifts and anointing

6. Health and strength

7. Favor

8. Protection from spiritual warfare

9. Ministry schedule - special prayer before, during and after specific assignments and meeting

10. Finances - personal and ministry

11. Increased revelation of truth

12. Open doors for utterance and effectual service

13. Praying the Scriptures over your leader has dynamic effect and influence

D.   CHARACTERISTICS OF A "PRAYER SHIELD INTERCESSOR"

1. Full of faith and stands on the integrity of the Word

2. Has a rich personal, devotional, and prayer life

3. Humble, meek and teachable spirit

4. Willing to be corrected when needed

5. Is in the light; has integrity

6. Able to keep a confidence

7. Is able to "birth" vision - knows how to pray through

8. Is discerning of battles and always prays through to victory

9. Committed and loyal to the leader they are praying for

10. Servant heart - does not usurp the leader's authority

11. A person of "no reputation"

12. Savior mentality - not critical or judgmental

13. Submits and handles prophetic revelation with proper protocol

    a. When receiving prophetic revelation, discerns if it is for prayer or if it is to be submitted

    b. If it is for submission, first submit it to the Prayer Shield Team Leader (if this is in place) for confirmation and direction

    c. If the prophetic insight contains a warning or a negative dimension to it, pray for the peace of the Lord and also for His word of victory to accompany it

    d. When submitting the revelation, does so in humility. The function of the prayer shield is to serve the leader with the prophetic revelation, not to rule them with it. Once it is submitted to them, it is the leader's responsibility before the Lord to respond to it.

    e. Be willing to be wrong. (We "prophesy in part" and it is possible to receive something with an inaccurate revelation or interpretation.

    f. Pray through the prophetic revelation.

E   **PRACTICAL HELPS IN SETTING UP A PRAYER SHIELD**

1. Be sensitive to the Spirit in setting up the team. A leader MUST be able to trust their prayer shied. Don't be hasty in choosing. You might want to have two or three different prayer shield teams for a leader.

   a. *Personal Intercessors* - this might be only a small number   (even 1 or 2) that are very loyal to the leader's call. The leader might confide in them concerning personal prayer needs. Confidentiality and loyalty are EXTREMELY important on this level.

   b. *Prayer Shield* - prays for the leader's ministry in fairly specific areas. Can be called on for crisis prayer.

   c. *General Prayer Team* - prays for general coverage of the leader but is not necessarily aware of any specifics.

2. Prayer Shield Team Leader. It is wise to assign a leader over the prayer shield team who will liaison with the ministry and the prayer shield team. This person will make sure prayer requests get out to the prayer shield; they will keep in touch with the leaders that they are are covering. Often, a Prayer Shield Team Leader can oversee a few prayer shields (for instance, if you have a number of ministry leaders in a church who need prayer shields, they could all be coordinated through one team leader).

3. Set-up. There are many different ways of coordinating and setting up a payer shield. Some will coordinate through e-mail or telephone. Others will host weekly meetings for the ministry leaders they are covering. As the Lord is sought concerning specific strategy, wisdom and creativity will be given.

F.   **THINGS TO CONSIDER**

1. Prayer shield intercessors are often forerunning in the battle and therefore take some of the spiritual assault that was intended for the leader. The prayer shield needs to continually secure the armor of God and walk in their authority. It is also wise for the prayer shield members to include the others on their team in prayer when they are praying for the leaders. Praying the Word of God over the leaders and the prayer shield is very powerful.

2. A prayer shield member needs to keep alert concerning their own walk with the Lord and their personal life. Sometimes spiritual assault can be subtle.... keep a check on things.

3. The two most damaging and hurtful things that are known to happen in prayer and prophetic circles are:

    a. Intercessors have on occasion been known to break their loyalty to the leader, and they criticize, judge or break confidence (i.e. Korah's rebellion).

    b. Intercessors have been known to usurp the vision of the leader with their own prophetic insights and interpretations (I.e. Miriam and Aaron, Korah, Absolom). Beware of falling prey to these things. A humble, servant attitude committed to the love of God will be the greatest safeguard.

4. NEVER pray negative prayers over your leader. All prayers must be unto edification, exhortation and comfort.

5. NEVER pray judgmental prayers over your leader. Always remember to maintain the heart of the Savior, not the judge.

G. SCRIPTURES TO PRAY OVER YOUR LEADERS

1. Devotional life and personal spiritual growth

    Philippians 1:6,9; Ephesians 1:15-19; 3:14-19; Colossians 1:9-12; Jude 24

2. Marriage and family

    Psalm 112; Proverbs 31:10-31; Acts 16:31; Isaiah 54:13

3. Ministry

    Isaiah 61:1-3; Ephesians 6:19; Romans 15:29; 2 Peter 1:2-4

4. Health and strength

    Psalm 103:1-5; 1 Peter 2:24; Isaiah 40:29-31

5. Favor

   Psalm 5:12

6. Wisdom

   James 1:5-6; 3-17-18; Ephesians 1:17; Proverbs 1:10

7. Provision

   Philippians 4:19; Deuteronomy 28:11-12; 3 John 2; Matthew 6:11

8. Warfare

   Psalm 91; Psalm 27; Psalm 23; Ephesians 6:10-17; John 4:4;Isaiah 54:17;
   Deuteronomy 28:7

—NOTES—

LESSON 13

PRAYER FOR HARVEST AND REVIVAL

1. **PRAYING FOR THE LOST**

    — **Ask the Lord to save lost souls and claim their salvation.**

    Psalm 2:8

    "Ask of Me, and I will surely give the nations as Your inheritance, and the very ends of the earth as Your possession."

    — **Bind the god of this world who has blinded them with unbelief.**

    2 Corinthians 4:3-4

    "And even if our gospel is veiled, it is veiled to those who are perishing, in whose case the god of this world has blinded the minds of the unbelieving so that they might not see the light of the gospel of the glory of Christ, who is the image of God."

    — **Take authority over any thoughts or imaginations raised up against truth.**

    2 Corinthians 10:4-5

    "For the weapons of our warfare are not of the flesh, but divinely powerful for the destruction of fortresses. We are destroying speculations and every lofty thing raised up against the knowledge of God, and we are taking every thought captive to the obedience of Christ."

    — **Pray for the conviction of the Holy Spirit.**

    John 16:8

    "And He, when He comes, will convict the world concerning sin and righteousness and judgment."

– **Claim repentance.**

Matthew 3:1-3

"John the Baptist came, preaching in the wilderness of Judea, saying, 'Repent, for the kingdom of heaven is at hand.' " (3:1-2)

"The voice of one crying in the wilderness, 'Make ready the way of the Lord. Make His paths straight!' "

– **Confess the remission of sins.**

John 20:23

"If you forgive the sins of any, their sins have been forgiven them; if you retain the sins of any, they have been retained."

– **Pray for believers to be sent to the lost to preach the Gospel.**

Matthew 9:38

"Therefore beseech the Lord of the harvest to send out workers into His harvest."

Mark 16:15

"And He said to them, "Go into all the world and preach the gospel to all creation."

– **Ask the Lord to surround His laborers with favor.**

Psalm 5:12

"For it is You who blesses the righteous man, O Lord, You surround him with favor as with a shield."

– **Pray that the seed (Word) will fall on good ground.**

Matthew 13:23

"And the one on whom seed was sown on the good soil, this is the man who hears the word and understands it; who indeed bears fruit and brings forth, some a hundredfold, some sixty, and some thirty."

—   **Ask the Holy Spirit to release faith.**

Ephesians 2:8

"For by grace you have been saved through faith; and that not of yourselves, it is the gift of God."

—   **Pray for a full revelation of Jesus Christ.**

Ephesians 1:17-18

"That the God of our Lord Jesus Christ, the Father of glory, may give to you a spirit of wisdom and of revelation in the knowledge of Him. I pray that the eyes of your heart may be enlightened, so that you will know what is the hope of His calling, what are the riches of the glory of His inheritance in the saints."

Ephesians 3:17-19

"So that Christ may dwell in your hearts through faith; and that you, being rooted and grounded in love, may be able to comprehend with all the saints what is the breadth and length and height and depth, and to know the love of Christ which surpasses knowledge, that you may be filled up to all the fullness of God."

—   **Pray for angels to be dispatched.**

Hebrews 1:14 (NKJV)

"Are they not all ministering spirits sent forth to minister for those who will inherit salvation?"

—   **Pray prophetic decrees.**

Genesis 1:1-3

"In the beginning God created the heavens and the earth. The earth was formless and void, and darkness was over the surface of the deep, and the Spirit of God was moving over the surface of the waters. Then God said, 'Let there be light' and there was light."

– **Pray in tongues for them.**

1 Corinthians 14:2

"For anyone who speaks in a tongue ... they utter mysteries by the Spirit." (NKJV)

– **Enter into travail as the Spirit leads.**

Isaiah 66:8

"Who has heard such a thing? Who has seen such things? Can a land be born in one day? Can a nation be brought forth all at once? As soon as Zion travailed, she also brought forth her sons."

– **Receive their salvation in your spirit by faith.**

Mark 11:24

"Therefore I say to you, all things for which you pray and ask, believe that you have received them, and they will be granted you."

– **Faith confessions and prayers of thanksgiving.**

Philippians 4:6

"Be anxious for nothing, but in everything by prayer and supplication with thanksgiving let your requests be made known to God."

2.   REVIVAL PRAYER

– **What is revival?**

Psalm 85:6

"Will You not Yourself revive us again, that Your people may rejoice in You?

Psalm 138:7

"Though I walk in the midst of trouble, You will revive me; You will stretch forth Your hand against the wrath of my enemies, and Your right hand will save me."

Isaiah 57:15

"For thus says the high and exalted One Who lives forever, whose name is Holy, 'I dwell on a high and holy place, and also with the contrite and lowly of spirit in order to revive the spirit of the lowly and to revive the heart of the contrite.' "

Ezra 9:9

"For we are slaves; yet in our bondage our God has not forsaken us, but has extended lovingkindness to us in the sight of the kings of Persia, to give us reviving to raise up the house of our God, to restore its ruins and to give us a wall."

John 10:10

"The thief comes only to steal and kill and destroy; I came that they may have life, and have it abundantly."

– **Hebrew "revive" = chayah = "to revive, keep (leave, make) alive, give promise of life, suffer to live, nourish up, preserve alive, quicken, recover, repair, restore, be whole"**

– **Greek "revive" =**

anathallo = "to flourish anew"

anazao = "to regain life, i.e., moral revival, to spring into activity"

3.   **WHY DOES THE BODY OF CHRIST NEED REVIVAL?**

The following symptoms often seen in the modern day church indicate a need for revival:

– Sin has separated us from God.

– Hardening of the heart

– Love growing cold

– Insensitivity to the Holy Spirit

    – Religious traditions

    – Disunity in the Body of Christ

    – Lack of manifestations of the power and the presence of God

4.   CAN DRY BONES LIVE?

    – Ezekiel 37:1-14

       • A need for prophetic vision

       • God's blueprint

       • God's faith

       • Man's obedience

5.   THE PRAYER OF IDENTIFICATION AND REPENTANCE

    – **Nehemiah**

Nehemiah 1:4-11

"I sat down and wept and mourned for days; and I was fasting and praying before the God of heaven." (1:4)

"I beseech You, O Lord God of heaven, the great and awesome God, who preserves the covenant and lovingkindness for those who love Him and keep His commandments." (1:5)

"Let Your ear now be attentive and Your eyes open to hear the prayer of Your servant which I am praying before You now, day and night, on behalf of the sons of Israel Your servants, confessing the sins of the sons of Israel which we have sinned against You; I and my father's house have sinned." (1:6)

"They are Your servants and Your people whom You redeemed by Your great power and by Your strong hand." (1:10)

"O Lord, I beseech You, may Your ear be attentive to the prayer of Your servant and the prayer of Your servants who delight to revere Your name, and make Your servant successful today." (1:11)

–   **Jesus**

•   In baptism

Matthew 3:13-17

"Then Jesus arrived from Galilee at the Jordan coming to John, to be baptized by him. But John tried to prevent Him, saying, 'I have need to be baptized by You, and do You come to me?' But Jesus answering said to him, 'Permit it at this time; for in this way it is fitting for us to fulfill
all righteousness.' Then he permitted Him. After being baptized, Jesus came up immediately from the water; and behold, the heavens were opened, and he saw the Spirit of God descending as a dove and lighting on Him, and behold, a voice out of the heavens said, 'This is My beloved Son, in whom I am well-pleased.' "

•   At the cross

Isaiah 53:6

"All of us like sheep have gone astray, each of us has turned to his own way; But the Lord has caused the iniquity of us all to fall on Him."

—NOTES—

ABOUT ROBERT HOTCHKIN

Minister, speaker and author, Robert Hotchkin is the founder of Men on the Frontlines and Robert Hotchkin Ministries. He also serves as one of the core leaders of Patricia King Ministries. Robert hosts the weekly Heroes Arise broadcast, and is a regular guest and co-host of Supernatural Life on God TV. His ministry and media inspire believers to grab hold of the finished work of the cross and walk in the fullness of their authority as Kingdom agents of impact. Robert is a passionate lover of Jesus Christ, and that passion is truly contagious! He ministers with strong faith, releasing revelation, prophetic decrees, healings, miracles, and the love of God. He is a true carrier of the glory and revival. People have been healed, refreshed, set free, and empowered through his life. He believes for heaven to impact lives and regions everywhere he goes.

—BOOKS—

LEVIATHAN EXPOSED

Overcoming the Hidden Schemes of a Demonic King. Leviathan is a high-level demonic spirit that works subtly behind the scenes to twist and pervert communications with the goal of destroying relationships and alliances. *Leviathan Exposed* offers the understanding, tools, and tactics you need to stop this demonic power in its tracks. Shut the door on its lies and manipulations to clear up communications, strengthen relationships, and get your destiny back on track.

REALMS OF POWER

Have you encountered a mighty touch from God that's left you wanting more? Good news! There is more! The Holy Spirit has opened up dimensions of supernatural power for your every need, just waiting to be unlocked! Broken down into revelatory, easy-to-read chapters—including practical steps for releasing new expressions of God's power in your every day life—*Realms of Power* will open your eyes to the dimensions of supernatural power that are meant to be a normal part of your life. It's time to uncover your true identity as a power-filled, born again believer in Jesus Christ. It's time to walk with a resolute understanding of the true power at work within you, so you can overcome any obstacle and move every mountain!

31 DECREES OF BLESSING FOR MEN

MASCULINITY IS UNDER ATTACK! Now more than ever, the world needs powerful men of faith and integrity. *31 Decrees of Blessing for Men* puts the power of God's Word in the hands and mouths of men, equipping them to be the husbands, fathers, brothers, leaders, and servants that God created them to be. You are a beloved son of God. You are a hero. Harness the power you have in Christ and become a blessing to the lives around you.

ABOUT ELVENA McCAIN

Elvena has ministered for over 30 years around the world serving as a missionary, teaching the gospel, ministering in healing and deliverance and leading intercession groups. She is an ordained minister and is currently ministering as a seasoned spiritual mentor to women of God, a core intercessor for Patricia King Ministries and Robert Hotchkin Ministries, a watchmen intercessor for Shiloh Fellowship Church and the Prayer Director for Extreme Love Ministries, a global ministry reaching the world with the word and love of God. Her passion is to bring change and activation to the body of Christ allowing them to step into their divine purpose, destiny and identity to advance the Kingdom of God.

—BOOK—

FAITH PLUNGE

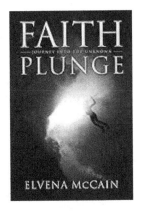

Do you shy away from uncertainties in your life? Do you lack the courage to say "yes" to situations that are unclear —or unknown? *Faith Plunge – Journey into the Unknown* brings a hopeful message to anyone unable or unwilling to face what is uncertain or unknown in any area of their life. The easy to read story format will bring encouragement and hope to all readers. The "keys' at the end of each chapter will enable you to activate your faith. Then, you may find yourself transitioning from fear to faith as you journey through each chapter. It's raw – it's real – it's true! Be encouraged to just jump in—and take your own FAITH PLUNGE!!!

—BOOKS BY PATRICIA KING—

EXPOSED - WITCHCRAFT IN THE CHURCH

Witchcraft in the church? Yes. It is operating in the church today, and many are suffering under its blatant and brutal assaults because there is lack of awareness. In *Exposed – Witchcraft in the Church,* Patricia King shares her personal journey with God as He has walked her through pathways of understanding, warfare encounters, and revelation on this subject over a forty-year period. It is a prophetic alert for the Body, offering enlightenment and creating hunger to grow in God's Kingdom authority and to be fearless in the face of any adversary.

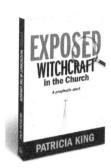

LIVE UNOFFENDABLE

No one has ever had more right to take offense over injustice, unrighteousness, and wickedness than Jesus. Yet, He never did. There are few things more anti-Christ and selfish than offense. It mires us in the what-about-me fowler's snare that hardens hearts and severely limits us from being able to represent the presence, power, and personality of our God in Whose image we are made. Patricia King's new book, *Live Unoffendable,* is potent and important. It will open your eyes (and your heart) to the dangers of offense and the subtle ways we often give place to it. It will also help you see the traps and limitations of offense.

31 DECREES OF BLESSING FOR WOMEN

Godly women are coming into greater places of influence in the world. The Holy Spirit is using them to prophesy life and send forth light through actions of compassion and justice. *31 Decrees of Blessing for Women* is especially designed to motivate women with a daily Scripture, an inspirational devotion, ten decrees, and empowering activations. Ignite God's Word in your heart and experience the multiplication of blessings as you are granted favor, extravagant generosity, unconditional love, fresh revelation, radiant beauty, and more.

—NOTES—